Discover

THE GOD OF
SECOND CHANCES

BASED ON THE PROPHET HOSEA

by
Brent and Diane Averill

FAITH
ALIVE®
Christian Resources

Grand Rapids, Michigan

Cover photo: PhotoDisc

Faith Alive Christian Resources published by CRC Publications. Discover Your Bible series. *Discover the God of Second Chances: Based on the Prophet Hosea* (Study Guide), © 2003 by CRC Publications, 2850 Kalamazoo Ave. SE, Grand Rapids, MI 49560. All rights reserved. With the exception of brief excerpts for review purposes, no part of this book may be reproduced in any manner whatsoever without written permission from the publisher. Printed in the United States of America on recycled paper.

We welcome your comments. Call us at 1-800-333-8300 or e-mail us at editors@faithaliveresources.org.

ISBN 1-59255-182-3

10 9 8 7 6 5 4 3 2 1

Contents

How to Study

The questions in this study booklet will help you discover for yourself what the Bible says. This is inductive Bible study—no one will tell you what the Bible says or what to believe. You will discover the message for yourself.

Questions are the key to inductive Bible study. Through questions you will search for the writers' thoughts and ideas. The prepared questions in this booklet are designed to help you in your quest for answers. You can and should ask your own questions too. The Bible comes alive with meaning for many people as they discover for themselves the exciting truths it contains. Our hope and prayer is that this booklet will help the Bible come alive for you.

The questions in this study are designed to be used with the New International Version of the Bible, but other translations can also be used.

Step 1. Read each Bible passage several times. Allow the thoughts and ideas to sink in. Think about its meaning. Ask questions of your own about the passage.

Step 2. Answer the questions, drawing your answers from the passage. Remember that the purpose of the study is to discover what the Bible says. Write your answers in your own words. If you use Bible study aids such as commentaries or Bible handbooks, do so only after completing your own personal study.

Step 3. Apply the Bible's message to your own life and world. Ask yourself these questions: What is this passage saying to me? How does it challenge me? Comfort me? Encourage me? Is there a promise I should claim? A warning I should heed? For what can I give thanks? If you sense God speaking to you in some way, respond to God in a personal prayer.

Step 4. Share your thoughts with someone else if possible. This will be easiest if you are part of a Bible study group that meets regularly to share discoveries and discuss questions. If you would like to learn of a study group in your area or if you would like more information on how to start a small group Bible study,

- write to Discover Your Bible at

2850 Kalamazoo Ave. SE	or	P.O. Box 5070
Grand Rapids, MI 49560		STN LCD 1
		Burlington, ON L7R 3Y8

- call toll-free 1-888-644-0814, e-mail *smallgroups@crcna.org*, or visit *www.SmallGroupMinistries.org* (for training advice and general information)

- call toll-free 1-800-333-8300 or visit *www.FaithAliveResources.org* (to order materials)

Introduction

In the book of Hosea we explore the deepest of human emotions and relationships. At one level, we encounter the intriguing story of a husband and wife, their difficult marriage, and the pain that spills over into the lives of their children. At another level we find the amazing story of God's faithful love for an unfaithful, hard-to-love people.

God calls Hosea to be a prophet in an unusual way. Hosea is to marry a prostitute who will be unfaithful to him. Hosea and his wife will also have children, who will suffer the painful effects of their mother's unfaithfulness. Through this experience, the prophet is able to record powerfully what happens when God's people reject him—and how God feels about it. Because Hosea is living the story, he learns how to portray God as a rejected lover, a forgiving husband, and a tender father. Through Hosea's eyes, we come to see that, no matter how imperfect our human relationships may be, there is One who loves, accepts, and forgives us beyond our wildest dreams. In fact, if we've ever thought of God as impersonal, unfeeling, or detached, we can see by this story how mistaken those notions are.

Although this study does not cover all the passages in Hosea's prophecy, the five lessons here include major themes from the book. The lessons also include several other Old Testament passages that fit thematically with the study material. And because Hosea's prophecy can serve as an introduction to God's grace in Jesus Christ, a number of New Testament passages enter in as well.

As you study this material, we pray that you will discover (anew or for the first time) the God of second chances, who so deeply loves us "that he gave his one and only Son, that whoever believes in him shall not perish but have eternal life" (John 3:16).

Glossary of Terms

Achor—a Hebrew word that means "troubling" (Hos. 2:15). The Valley of Achor gets its name from being the place where an Israelite is punished for sinning against God during the battle of Jericho (Josh. 7:24-26).

Admah—a city that was destroyed along with Sodom and Gomorrah (Gen. 19:24-25; Deut. 29:23).

Ahaz—a king of Judah from 735-715 B.C.

Assyria—a powerful empire during the eighth century B.C. Assyria's armies conquered the ten northern tribes of Israel and took them away into exile around 721 B.C.

Baals—Canaanite fertility gods, believed to have influence over agriculture, livestock, and human sexuality. The chief god was also called Hadad; any idol named for him was called a Baal.

betrothal—the promise of marriage.

church—the New Testament (new covenant) people of God; also called the body of Christ, who is its head; Christ loves and cares for the church as a faithful husband should love and care for his wife (Eph. 1:22-23; 4:15-16; 5:25-33).

covenant—a mutually binding agreement in which the parties agree to certain responsibilities. Under the old covenant, before Christ, God promised to care for and bless the people of Israel if they would obey God's law and worship God alone (Ex. 24:3-7; Deut. 4-6; 28-30). Under the new covenant, instituted by Jesus, who came to fulfill the old covenant, God's people are all who believe in Jesus Christ as Savior and Lord (Gen. 12:1-3; Matt. 5:17; Luke 22:20; Gal. 3:26-29).

denarii, denarius—a denarius was a Roman coin worth about a day's wages in the first century A.D.

Ephraim—One of the largest and strongest of the twelve tribes of Israel. After the split of the kingdom in about 930 B.C. into ten northern tribes and two southern tribes, the name *Ephraim* was sometimes used to refer to the ten northern tribes together. (The name *Israel* was more commonly used to refer to those tribes.)

Gomer—a prostitute who became Hosea's wife.

Hezekiah—a king of Judah from 715-686 B.C.

Holy One of God—a reference to the promised Messiah who would come to usher in God's everlasting kingdom of righteousness.

homer—(also called a cor) a volume measurement in ancient Israel, equal to about six bushels (220 liters).

hope—refers to looking ahead to the full life God promises, and living for God with that view in mind.

Hosea—a prophet in Israel who lived in the eighth century B.C. He prophesied from around 755-715 B.C.

Israel—the name commonly used in the Bible to refer to God's chosen people, the descendants of Jacob (whom God renamed Israel—Gen. 32:28). This name originally included all twelve tribes descended from the sons of Jacob, but after 930 B.C., when the kingdom of Israel split into ten northern tribes and two southern tribes, the name usually referred to the ten northern tribes.

Jeroboam—(also known as Jeroboam II) a king of Israel from 793-753 B.C.

Jezreel—Hosea and Gomer's first child, a son. This name, which in Hebrew means "God scatters," is also the name of a city where King Jehu of Israel (841-814 B.C.) massacred the family of Ahab (2 Kings 9-10).

Jotham—a king of Judah from 750-732 B.C.

Judah—the name commonly used to refer to the two southern tribes (Judah and Benjamin) of the divided kingdom of Israel.

justice—just and right treatment for all, in line with God's way for living; closely linked to righteousness.

lethek—a volume measurement in ancient Israel, equal to about three bushels (110 liters).

Lo-Ammi—Hosea and Gomer's third child, a son. In Hebrew this name means "not my people."

Lo-Ruhamah—Hosea and Gomer's second child, a daughter. In Hebrew this name means "not pitied" or "not loved."

Peter—(sometimes called Simon Peter) one of Jesus' twelve disciples (apostles); a close friend of Jesus, he often spoke as the disciples' leader.

raisin cakes—a thank offering baked in the name of Baal for a plentiful harvest.

righteousness—right living in God's sight; life in perfect harmony with God, with other people, and with God's world; comes from the same root word as *justice*. When we repent of our sins and trust in Jesus as Lord and Savior, God sees us as having the righteousness of Christ (Rom. 3:21-26).

shekel—a unit of weight in ancient Israel, equal to about two-fifths of an ounce (11.5 grams).

the Twelve—Jesus' twelve specially chosen disciples, also known as the twelve apostles (Luke 6:12-16).

Uzziah—(also named Azariah) a king of Judah from 792-740 B.C.

world—In the New Testament this word often refers to people or systems of this world that do not follow Jesus.

Zeboiim—a city (like Admah) that was destroyed along with Sodom and Gomorrah (Gen. 19:24-25; Deut. 29:23).

Lesson 1

Hosea 1:1-2:1; Jeremiah 3:14-15; 1 Peter 2:9-10

A Marriage Made in Heaven

Introductory Notes

A young woman came to a Bible study one morning. One of the women in the group had kept inviting her, and in order to get this friend off her back, she had finally agreed to come.

It was obvious that she didn't want to be there, but it was exactly where she needed to be. She was a young mother with three small children, and her husband had left her when he learned that she had been diagnosed with cancer. The whole time she was at the Bible study she gave the impression that she did not want to be there. She was angry at her unfaithful husband, and she was angry at God. The other women there were kind to her and indicated they would try to help in any way, but she made clear that she was going to fight her troubles on her own. She figured she did not need her husband, other people, or God. Occasionally she would be seen at the hospital while she was having treatments, but she always kept people from the Bible study at arm's length.

Then about three years later one of the group members received a call saying that the young woman was dying and was asking if someone could come and talk with her. As her friend from the Bible study walked into the room, the first words out of her mouth were "Why did God do this to me? Why am I dying of cancer and leaving three small children?"

Because she was in intensive care, there were only a few moments to tell her the most important thing she would ever hear. Her visitor said that none of us could say why she got cancer and other people did not. But, more important, she needed to know that God loved her enough to send his Son into this world to die for her. In her moment of desperation she had to understand that even if her husband had been unfaithful, God had not been. In fact, she had to admit that by trying to live life on her own, *she* had been unfaithful—unfaithful to God. After this, her visitor explained what it meant to ask Jesus into her heart. The dying woman leaned back and between deep breaths of oxygen she said, "I understand." What a blessing it was that she could receive the God who said to her in her darkest hour, "You are my loved one; you are one of my people."

1. *Hosea 1:1-3*

   ¹*The word of the* L*ORD* *that came to Hosea son of Beeri during the reigns of Uzziah, Jotham, Ahaz and Hezekiah, kings of Judah, and during the reign of Jeroboam son of Jehoash king of Israel:*

   ²*When the* L*ORD* *began to speak through Hosea, the* L*ORD* *said to him, "Go, take to yourself an adulterous wife and children of unfaithfulness, because the land is guilty of the vilest adultery in departing from the* L*ORD*.*" *³*So he married Gomer daughter of Diblaim, and she conceived and bore him a son.*

   a. Comment on the unusual call God gave to Hosea. Why do you think the author tells precisely when Hosea became a prophet?

   b. Why do you think God tells Hosea to marry an adulterous woman? How would that affect Hosea as a prophet?

2. *Hosea 1:4-9*

   ⁴*Then the* L*ORD* *said to Hosea, "Call him Jezreel, because I will soon punish the house of Jehu for the massacre at Jezreel, and I will put an end to the kingdom of Israel. ⁵In that day I will break Israel's bow in the Valley of Jezreel."*

   ⁶*Gomer conceived again and gave birth to a daughter. Then the* L*ORD* *said to Hosea, "Call her Lo-Ruhamah, for I will no longer show love to the house of Israel, that I should at all forgive them. ⁷Yet I will show love to the house of Judah; and I will save them—not by bow, sword or battle, or by horses and horsemen, but by the* L*ORD* *their God."*

   ⁸*After she had weaned Lo-Ruhamah, Gomer had another son. ⁹Then the* L*ORD* *said, "Call him Lo-Ammi, for you are not my people, and I am not your God."*

   a. What's the significance of each of the children's names?

b.   How do these names, indicating God's judgment, fit with the idea that God is loving?

3.   *Hosea 1:10-2:1*

   [10]*"Yet the Israelites will be like the sand on the seashore, which cannot be measured or counted. In the place where it was said to them, 'You are not my people,' they will be called 'sons of the living God.'* [11]*The people of Judah and the people of Israel will be reunited, and they will appoint one leader and will come up out of the land, for great will be the day of Jezreel.*

   [1]*"Say of your brothers, 'My people,' and of your sisters, 'My loved one.'"*

a.   What promise is God giving here?

b.   Who might be the leader described in verse 11?

4.   *Jeremiah 3:14-15*

   [14]*"Return, faithless people," declares the* LORD, *"for I am your husband. I will choose you—one from a town and two from a clan—and bring you to Zion.* [15]*Then I will give you shepherds after my own heart, who will lead you with knowledge and understanding."*

a.   How does God describe himself in this passage?

b.   Who is God's spouse, and what does God want in this relationship?

c.   What seems to be the function of the shepherds mentioned in this passage?

5.   *1 Peter 2:9-10*

⁹. . . You are a chosen people, a royal priesthood, a holy nation, a people belonging to God, that you may declare the praises of him who called you out of darkness into his wonderful light. ¹⁰Once you were not a people, but now you are the people of God; once you had not received mercy, but now you have received mercy.

a.   What does it mean to belong to God?

b.   What are the people who belong to God called to do?

Questions for Reflection

How does the analogy of a faithful husband alter or enhance your view of God?

What promises does God make to you when you are (figuratively) like Gomer?

Lesson 2
Hosea 2:2-7; 3:1-3; Luke 7:36-50

Love Means Having to Say You're Sorry

Introductory Notes

In John Grisham's book *The Testament,* the main character has made a mess of his life. He's a lawyer who's had two failed marriages, many affairs, and an alcohol addiction that he can't kick. He is plucked out of rehab by his law firm and asked to go to South America to find a woman missionary doctor who has inherited a huge fortune. He discovers this woman deep in the Brazilian jungle working with a small native tribe, and, amazingly, she is not interested in the money. Deeply affected by this woman and her love for God, the lawyer also discovers his own need for faith.

After a serious bout with a tropical disease, he finds his way to a small church and admits that he's made a mess of his life. Grisham describes the scene this way:

> Nate closed his eyes . . . and called God's name. God was waiting. With both hands, he clenched the back of the pew in front of him. . . . Mumbling softly [he listed] every weakness and flaw and affliction and evil that plagued him. He confessed them all in one long glorious acknowledgment of failure, he laid himself bare before God. He held nothing back. He unloaded enough burdens to crush any three men, and when he finally finished Nate had tears in his eyes. "I'm sorry," he whispered to God. "Please help me."

1. *Hosea 2:2*

   ²*"Rebuke your mother, rebuke her, for she is not my wife, and I am not her husband. Let her remove the adulterous look from her face and the unfaithfulness from between her breasts."*

   a. Whom does Hosea ask to join him in showing "tough love" to Gomer, and what will be the effect?

b. Explain how this approach might work for family intervention purposes today.

c. On a different level, what is God saying symbolically to his people in these verses?

2. *Hosea 2:3-5*

[3]*"Otherwise I will strip her naked and make her as bare as on the day she was born; I will make her like a desert, turn her into a parched land, and slay her with thirst. [4]I will not show my love to her children, because they are the children of adultery. [5]Their mother has been unfaithful and has conceived them in disgrace. She said, 'I will go after my lovers, who give me my food and my water, my wool and my linen, my oil and my drink.'"*

a. While it is not necessary to understand these verses in a literal sense or in a way that condones abuse, what desperate measures is Hosea willing to take?

b. What would drive Hosea to react this way?

3. *Hosea 2:6-7*

[6]*"Therefore I will block her path with thornbushes; I will wall her in so that she cannot find her way. [7]She will chase after her lovers but not catch them; she will look for them but not find them. Then she will say, 'I will go back to my husband as at first, for then I was better off than now.'"*

a.   What does Hosea plan to do?

b.   What kind of a response does Hosea hope to get from Gomer?

c.   What considerations would motivate Gomer's return to Hosea? A sinful people's return to God?

4. *Hosea 3:1-3*

    ¹*The* LORD *said to me, "Go, show your love to your wife again, though she is loved by another and is an adulteress. Love her as the* LORD *loves the Israelites, though they turn to other gods and love the sacred raisin cakes." ²So I bought her for fifteen shekels of silver and about a homer and a lethek of barley. ³Then I told her, "You are to live with me many days; you must not be a prostitute or be intimate with any man, and I will live with you."*

    a.   What is Hosea told to do? Why is this a difficult request?

    b.   Describe the conditions that will permit Gomer to return home.

5. *Luke 7:36-50*

    ³⁶*Now one of the Pharisees invited Jesus to have dinner with him, so he went to the Pharisee's house and reclined at the table. ³⁷When a woman who had lived a sinful life in that town learned that Jesus was eating at the Pharisee's*

house, she brought an alabaster jar of perfume, [38]and as she stood behind him at his feet weeping, she began to wet his feet with her tears. Then she wiped them with her hair, kissed them and poured perfume on them.

[39]When the Pharisee who had invited him saw this, he said to himself, "If this man were a prophet, he would know who is touching him and what kind of woman she is—that she is a sinner."

[40]Jesus answered him, "Simon, I have something to tell you."

"Tell me, teacher," he said.

[41]"Two men owed money to a certain moneylender. One owed him five hundred denarii, and the other fifty. [42]Neither of them had the money to pay him back, so he canceled the debts of both. Now which of them will love him more?"

[43]Simon replied, "I suppose the one who had the bigger debt canceled."

"You have judged correctly," Jesus said.

[44]Then he turned toward the woman and said to Simon, "Do you see this woman? I came into your house. You did not give me any water for my feet, but she wet my feet with her tears and wiped them with her hair. [45]You did not give me a kiss, but this woman, from the time I entered, has not stopped kissing my feet. [46]You did not put oil on my head, but she has poured perfume on my feet. [47]Therefore, I tell you, her many sins have been forgiven—for she loved much. But he who has been forgiven little loves little."

[48]Then Jesus said to her, "Your sins are forgiven."

[49]The other guests began to say among themselves, "Who is this who even forgives sins?"

[50]Jesus said to the woman, "Your faith has saved you; go in peace."

a.   Compare and contrast the woman in Luke with Gomer.

b.   From both of these stories what do we find that the characters need to recognize about themselves?

Question for Reflection

What do we learn about repentance and love in this lesson?

Lesson 3
Hosea 2:14-23; Jeremiah 31:31-34; Ephesians 5:25-33

True Romance

Introductory Notes

A story of unconditional love can be compelling. While the main theme of the book of Hosea focuses on the love of God for his people, the book also portrays Hosea as a husband being encouraged to love his wife in spite of her rejection of him. Christian author Francine Rivers has written a novel based on these themes. In that story, titled *Redeeming Love*, a man chooses to marry a woman although she is a prostitute. His love is compelling because of the lengths he goes to maintain his love for her. In fact, his love for her does not seem natural—and it is not. A love that first reaches out to the unlovely is the kind of love God gives us—and that is not natural for us; it is supernatural.

1. Hosea 2:14-17

14"Therefore [says the LORD] I am now going to allure her; I will lead her into the desert and speak tenderly to her. 15There I will give her back her vineyards, and will make the Valley of Achor a door of hope. There she will sing as in the days of her youth, as in the day she came up out of Egypt.

16"In that day," declares the LORD, "you will call me 'my husband'; you will no longer call me 'my master.' 17I will remove the names of the Baals from her lips; no longer will their names be invoked."

Note: The imagery in this passage pictures the relationship of an unfaithful wife to her faithful, caring husband. While the primary, or "big-picture," application centers on the relationship of a caring and loving God to an unfaithful people, the personal relationship of Hosea to Gomer remains part of the context as well. So both levels of relationship enter in as we explore and discuss this passage.

a. How does God treat Israel, and how does Hosea decide to treat Gomer?

b.   What do you think the response will be to this kind of love?

c.   Because this passage also describes God's treatment of us, what should be our response to God?

2.   **Hosea 2:18-23**

   ¹⁸*In that day I will make a covenant for them with the beasts of the field and the birds of the air and the creatures that move along the ground. Bow and sword and battle I will abolish from the land, so that all may lie down in safety.* ¹⁹*I will betroth you to me forever; I will betroth you in righteousness and justice, in love and compassion.* ²⁰*I will betroth you in faithfulness, and you will acknowledge the LORD.*

   ²¹*"In that day I will respond," declares the LORD—"I will respond to the skies, and they will respond to the earth;* ²²*and the earth will respond to the grain, the new wine and oil, and they will respond to Jezreel.* ²³*I will plant her for myself in the land; I will show my love to the one I called 'Not my loved one.' I will say to those called 'Not my people,' 'You are my people'; and they will say, 'You are my God.'"*

a.   List some of the promises that God as husband makes to his "bride."

b.   What will be the expected results?

3.   **Jeremiah 31:31-34**

   ³¹*"The time is coming," declares the LORD, "when I will make a new covenant with the house of Israel and with the house of Judah.* ³²*It will not be like the covenant I made with their forefathers when I took them by the hand to*

lead them out of Egypt, because they broke my covenant, though I was a husband to them," declares the LORD.

³³"This is the covenant I will make with the house of Israel after that time," declares the LORD. "I will put my law in their minds and write it on their hearts. I will be their God, and they will be my people. ³⁴No longer will a man teach his neighbor, or a man his brother, saying, 'Know the LORD,' because they will all know me, from the least of them to the greatest," declares the LORD. "For I will forgive their wickedness and will remember their sins no more."

a. What additional promises does God make in this passage from Jeremiah?

b. Explain what it means to know the Lord.

c. What do we learn about forgiveness in these verses?

4. Ephesians 5:25-33

²⁵Husbands, love your wives, just as Christ loved the church and gave himself up for her ²⁶to make her holy, cleansing her by the washing with water through the word, ²⁷and to present her to himself as a radiant church, without stain or wrinkle or any other blemish, but holy and blameless. ²⁸In this same way, husbands ought to love their wives as their own bodies. He who loves his wife loves himself. ²⁹After all, no one ever hated his own body, but he feeds and cares for it, just as Christ does the church—³⁰for we are members of his body. ³¹"For this reason a man will leave his father and mother and be united to his wife, and the two will become one flesh." ³²This is a profound mystery—but I am talking about Christ and the church. ³³However, each one of you also must love his wife as he loves himself, and the wife must respect her husband.

a. What model for human relationships do we see in this passage?

b. What kind of love is described in these verses?

Question for Reflection

How can God help us in our closest relationships?

Lesson 4
Hosea 11:1-4, 8-11; Matthew 18:12-14; 1 John 3:1-3

Family Ties

Introductory Notes

In a collection of stories about fathers, titled *Thanks, Dad, for Teaching Me Well,* psychologist Larry Crabb describes what is often the connection between our view of earthly dads and our view of our heavenly Father:

> For many people the word *father* connotes bad memories. In their emotional thesaurus, it means one who abandons, abuses, demeans, and demands perfection. Small wonder that fathers all too often represent obstacles, not avenues, to embracing the concept of God as Father. For me the word *father* brings to mind the best of memories. For me it is an avenue, for I have been drawn to love God by my father.

1. Hosea 11:1-4

[1]*"When Israel was a child, I loved him, and out of Egypt I called my son.* [2]*But the more I called Israel, the further they went from me. They sacrificed to the Baals and they burned incense to images.* [3]*It was I who taught Ephraim to walk, taking them by the arms; but they did not realize it was I who healed them.* [4]*I led them with cords of human kindness, with ties of love; I lifted the yoke from their neck and bent down to feed them."*

a. How is God portrayed in these verses?

b. Even with God's gracious treatment, how did the "children" respond?

2.   *Hosea 11:8-9*

   [8]*"How can I give you up, Ephraim? How can I hand you over, Israel? How can I treat you like Admah? How can I make you like Zeboiim? My heart is changed within me; all my compassion is aroused.* [9]*I will not carry out my fierce anger, nor will I turn and devastate Ephraim. For I am God, and not man—the Holy One among you. I will not come in wrath."*

   a.   What picture of God emerges from the questions in this passage?

   b.   What does God mean by saying, "I am . . . not man?"

3.   *Hosea 11:10-11*

   [10]*"They will follow the* LORD*; he will roar like a lion. When he roars, his children will come trembling from the west.* [11]*They will come trembling like birds from Egypt, like doves from Assyria. I will settle them in their homes,"* declares the LORD*."*

   a.   What does the imagery of a lion convey, and what does this have to do with God?

   b.   What kind of response does God want from his people?

   c.   What do you think it means that God will settle the people in their homes?

4. Matthew 18:12-14

[12]*"What do you think? If a man owns a hundred sheep, and one of them wanders away, will he not leave the ninety-nine on the hills and go to look for the one that wandered off?* [13]*And if he finds it, I tell you the truth, he is happier about that one sheep than about the ninety-nine that did not wander off.* [14]*In the same way your Father in heaven is not willing that any of these little ones should be lost."*

a. What is Jesus saying in this parable?

b. What do we learn here about God's care for individuals? About the kind of care we should give others?

5. 1 John 3:1-3

[1]*How great is the love the Father has lavished on us, that we should be called children of God! And that is what we are! The reason the world does not know us is that it did not know him.* [2]*Dear friends, now we are children of God, and what we will be has not yet been made known. But we know that when he appears, we shall be like him, for we shall see him as he is.* [3]*Everyone who has this hope in him purifies himself, just as he is pure.*

a. How are people who believe in God described in this passage?

b. Why does the world not know us?

c. In the light of this Scripture passage, how should we see ourselves?

Question for Reflection

In what ways does our view of an earthly father affect the way we view God?

Lesson 5

Hosea 6:1-3; 10:12; 14:1-9; Isaiah 1:18; John 6:66-69

Coming to One's Senses

Introductory Notes

A Severe Mercy is a beautiful love story written by Sheldon Vanauken. In it he tells the story of his love for his wife, Jean, or "Davy," as he called her. Early in their relationship they set up what they called "the shining barrier." It was a commitment to actively resist anything that would keep their love from deepening.

For a number of years this barrier worked in spite of their seeing God as irrelevant to their lives. But while Sheldon was at graduate school in England, they became friends with some Christian students and began to look at the claims of Christianity. They both decided to pursue a relationship with God through faith in Jesus, and they found that only God could perfectly love them. Once they discovered that all human love, including their love for each other, was imperfect, their love deepened even more.

God is the One who seeks us first and loves us perfectly. And we need to respond. It only makes sense to choose God, who has chosen us. God alone has the words of eternal life. The Scriptures for this lesson teach us that we need to come to our senses in our relationship with God.

1. **Hosea 6:1-3**

    [1]*"Come, let us return to the LORD. He has torn us to pieces but he will heal us; he has injured us but he will bind up our wounds.* [2]*After two days he will revive us; on the third day he will restore us, that we may live in his presence.* [3]*Let us acknowledge the LORD; let us press on to acknowledge him. As surely as the sun rises, he will appear; he will come to us like the winter rains, like the spring rains that water the earth."*

    a. What are the people of Israel asked to do in this passage?

b. How and when should we return to the Lord?

c. What does it mean to acknowledge God?

2. **Hosea 10:12**

Sow for yourselves righteousness, reap the fruit of unfailing love, and break up your unplowed ground; for it is time to seek the LORD, until he comes and showers righteousness on you.

a. What does it mean to sow righteousness?

b. What is the result of sowing righteousness?

3. **Hosea 14:1-9**

[1]Return, O Israel, to the LORD your God. Your sins have been your downfall! [2]Take words with you and return to the LORD. Say to him: "Forgive all our sins and receive us graciously, that we may offer the fruit of our lips. [3]Assyria cannot save us; we will not mount war-horses. We will never again say 'Our gods' to what our own hands have made, for in you the fatherless find compassion."

[4]"I will heal their waywardness and love them freely, for my anger has turned away from them. [5]I will be like the dew to Israel; he will blossom like a lily. Like a cedar of Lebanon he will send down his roots; [6]his young shoots will grow. His splendor will be like an olive tree, his fragrance like a cedar of Lebanon. [7]Men will dwell again in his shade. He will flourish like the grain. He will blossom like a vine, and his fame will be like the wine from Lebanon.

⁸O Ephraim, what more have I to do with idols? I will answer him and care for him. I am like a green pine tree; your fruitfulness comes from me."

⁹Who is wise? He will realize these things. Who is discerning? He will understand them. The ways of the LORD are right; the righteous walk in them, but the rebellious stumble in them.

a. What words should the people of Israel speak to God if they wish to return to God?

b. What images in Hosea 14 describe the way God would bring restoration to the people?

c. Contrast the righteous person and the rebellious person.

4. Isaiah 1:18

"Come now, let us reason together," says the LORD. "Though your sins are like scarlet, they shall be as white as snow; though they are red as crimson, they shall be like wool."

a. How would you describe the process of God's forgiveness?

b. What does the change from scarlet to white imply?

5. *John 6:66-69*

> *[66]From this time many of [Jesus'] disciples turned back and no longer followed him.*
> *[67]"You do not want to leave too, do you?" Jesus asked the Twelve.*
> *[68]Simon Peter answered him, "Lord, to whom shall we go? You have the words of eternal life. [69]We believe and know that you are the Holy One of God."*

    a.   Why do you think Jesus asked his disciples whether they wished to leave him?

    b.   What appear to be the main reasons the disciples stayed with Jesus?

Questions for Reflection

What does it mean for us to come to our senses?

How would you now explain to someone that God is the God of second chances?

An Invitation

Listen now to what God is saying to you.

You may be aware of things in your life that keep you from coming near to God. You may have thought of God as unsympathetic, angry, and punishing. You may feel as if you don't know how to pray or how to come near to God.

"But because of his great love for us, God, who is rich in mercy, made us alive with Christ even when we were dead in transgressions—it is by grace you have been saved" (Eph. 2:4). Jesus, God's Son, died on the cross to save us from our sins. It doesn't matter where you come from, what you've done in the past, or what your heritage is. None of these things makes any difference to God. God has been watching over you and caring for you, drawing you closer. "And you also were included in Christ when you heard the word of truth, the gospel of your salvation" (1:13). So now accept God's invitation to become his adopted child through Jesus Christ. It's as simple as A-B-C:

- **A**dmit that you have sinned and that you need God's forgiveness.
- **B**elieve that God loves you and that Jesus already paid the price for your sins.
- **C**ommit your life to God in prayer, asking God to forgive your sins, make you his child, and fill you with the Holy Spirit.

Prayer of Commitment

Here is a prayer of commitment to Jesus Christ as Savior. If you long to be in a loving relationship with Jesus, pray this prayer. If you have already committed your life to Jesus, use this prayer for renewal and praise.

Dear God, I come to you simply and honestly to confess that I have sinned, that sin is a part of who I am. And yet I know that you listen to sinners who are truthful before you. So I come with empty hands and heart, asking for forgiveness.

I confess that only through faith in Jesus Christ can I come to you. I confess my need for a Savior, and I thank you, Jesus, for dying on the cross to pay the price for my sins. Lord, I ask that you forgive my sins and count me among those who are righteous in your sight. Remove the guilt that accompanies sin and bring me into your presence.

Holy Spirit of God, help me to pray, and teach me to live by your Word. Faithful God, help me to serve you faithfully. Make me more and more like Jesus each day, and help me to share with others the good news of your great salvation. In Jesus' name, Amen.

Recommended Reading

Averill, Brent and Diane. *So You've Been Asked to Share Your Faith*. Grand Rapids, Mich.: Faith Alive, 2001.

Boice, James M. *The Minor Prophets*. Grand Rapids, Mich.: Kregel, 1996.

Gire, Ken. *Thanks, Dad, for Teaching Me Well*. Colorado Springs, Colo.: Waterbrook, 1999.

Grisham, John. *The Testament*. New York: Doubleday, 1999.

Gumbel, Nicky. *Why Jesus?* New York: Alpha North America, 1991.

Lewis, C. S. *The Lion, the Witch, and The Wardrobe*. New York: Macmillan, 1950.

Marshall, I. Howard. *The Epistles of John*. Grand Rapids, Mich.: Eerdmans, 1978.

Oswalt, John N. *The Book of Isaiah: Chapters 1-39*. Grand Rapids, Mich.: Eerdmans, 1986.

Rivers, Francine. *Redeeming Love*. Sisters, Ore.: Multnomah, 1997.

Stuart, Douglas. *Word Biblical Commentary: Hosea-Jonah*. Waco, Tex.: Word, 1987.

Thompson, J. A. *The Book of Jeremiah*. Grand Rapids, Mich.: Eerdmans, 1980.

Vanauken, Sheldon. *A Severe Mercy*. San Francisco: Harper, 1992.

Young, Edward J. *The Book of Isaiah*. Grand Rapids, Mich.: Eerdmans, 1992.

Evaluation Questionnaire

DISCOVER THE GOD OF SECOND CHANCES:
BASED ON THE PROPHET HOSEA

As you complete this study, please fill out this questionnaire to help us evaluate the effectiveness of our materials. Please be candid. Thank you.

1. Was this a home group ___ or a church-based ___ program? What church?

2. Was the study used for
   ___ a community evangelism group?
   ___ a community grow group?
   ___ a church Bible study group?

3. How would you rate the materials?

   Study Guide
   ___ excellent ___ very good ___ good ___ fair ___ poor

   Leader Guide
   ___ excellent ___ very good ___ good ___ fair ___ poor

4. What were the strengths?

5. What were the weaknesses?

6. What would you suggest to improve the material?

7. In general, what was the experience of your group?

Your name (optional)_____

Address _____

_____

8. Other comments:

(Please fold, tape, stamp, and mail. Thank you.)

Faith Alive Christian Resources
2850 Kalamazoo Ave. SE
Grand Rapids, MI 49560